HE IS RISEN

Rocks Tell the Story of Easter

For God so loved the world
that He gave His only begotten Son,
that whoever believes in Him should not perish
but have everlasting life.

John 3:16

ZONDERVAN

He is Risen: Rocks Tell the Story of Easter
Copyright © 2019 by Patti Rokus
Photos © 2019 Patti Rokus

Requests for information should be addressed to:
Zondervan, 3900 Sparks Dr. SE, Grand Rapids, Michigan 49546

Library of Congress Cataloging-in-Publication Data

Names: Rokus, Patti, 1967- author.
Title: He is risen : rocks tell the story of Easter / Patti Rokus.
Description: Grand Rapids : Zonderkidz, 2019. |
Identifiers: LCCN 2018030206 (print) | LCCN 2018042620 (ebook) | ISBN 9780310764915 |
    ISBN 9780310764861 (hardcover)
Subjects: LCSH: Jesus Christ—Biography—Passion Week—Juvenile literature. | Holy Week—
    Juvenile literature.
Classification: LCC BT414 (ebook) | LCC BT414 .R65 2019 (print) | DDC 232.96—dc23
LC record available at https://lccn.loc.gov/2018030206

All Scripture quotations are taken from the New King James Version® (NKJV).
© 1982 by Thomas Nelson. Used by permission. All rights reserved.

Interior design: Patti Rokus

Printed in China

---

22 23 24 /DSC/ 22 21 20 19 18 17 16 15 14 13 12 11 10 9 8 7 6 5 4 3

Jesus loves me.

We love Him
because He first loved us.

1 John 4:19

Jesus came to earth
to bring us healing and joy,
and to lead us back home to God.

These things I have spoken to you, that in Me you may have peace. In the world you will have tribulation; but be of good cheer, I have overcome the world.

John 16:33

The last week of
His mortal life was the
most important week
ever.

"'Blessed is the King who comes in the name of the LORD!' Peace in heaven and glory in the highest!"

Luke 19:38

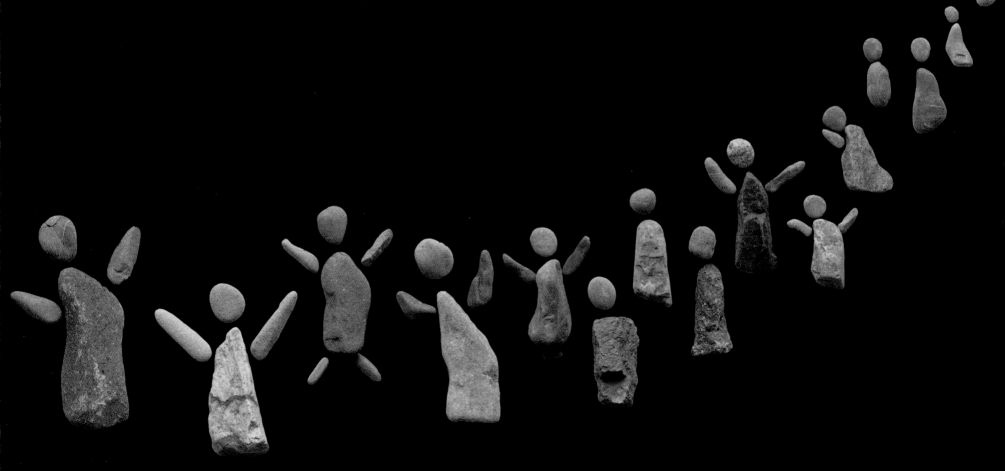

Many people celebrated Him as the Savior.

The whole multitude of the disciples began to rejoice and praise God with a loud voice for all the mighty works they had seen.

Luke 19:37

But some people wanted to kill Him.

From that day on, they plotted to put Him to death.

John 11:53

One friend betrayed Him.

Jesus said, "Assuredly, I say to you, one of you . . . will betray Me."

Mark 14:18

Before Jesus died,
He taught His friends
important lessons
at His last supper.

Love and serve one another.

He poured water into a basin and began to wash the disciples' feet.

John 13:5

Eat and drink in remembrance of Me.

"This is My body which is given for you . . .
This cup is the new covenant in My blood, which is shed for you."

Luke 22:19–20

Then He prayed in a garden,
taking upon Himself
all our pain and sorrows,
so we can let them go.

"My soul is exceedingly sorrowful, even to death."

Mark 14:34

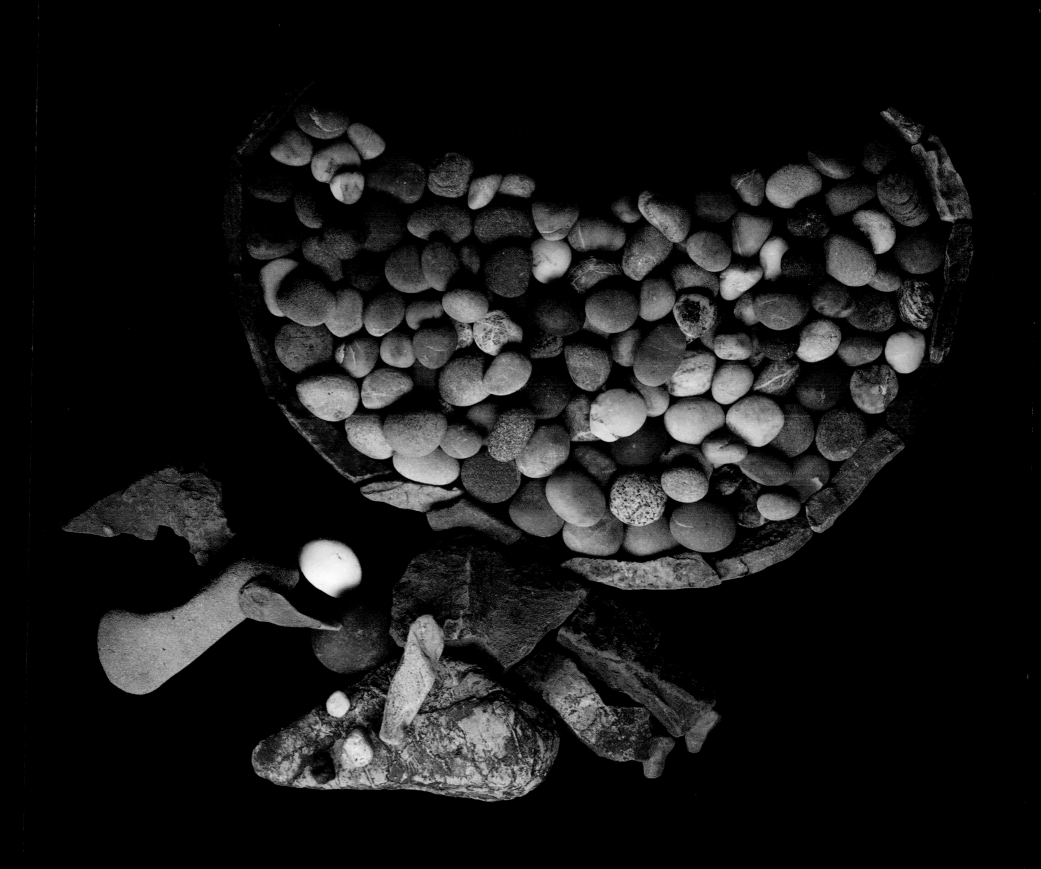

Jesus willingly
gave His life on the cross.

He paid the price for our sins,

to rescue us and bring us home.

"He has borne our griefs and carried our sorrows . . .
He was wounded for our transgressions . . .
And by His stripes we are healed."

Isaiah 53:4–5

He was buried in a tomb.

Then [Joseph of Arimathea] bought fine linen, took Him down, and wrapped Him in the linen.
And he laid Him in a tomb which had been hewn out of the rock.

Mark 15:46

After three days,

Jesus came back to life!

We will all live again because

He conquered death.

*"I am the resurrection and the life.
He who believes in Me, though he
may die, he shall live."*

John 11:25

Alive again,
Jesus visited His friends.

Jesus Himself stood in the midst of them, and said to them, "Peace to you . . . Behold My hands and My feet."

Luke 24:36, 39

He asked His friends to share the good news.

"Feed My lambs . . .
Tend My sheep."

John 21:15–16

Jesus went to heaven.

"Why do you stand gazing up into heaven? This same Jesus, who was taken up from you into heaven, will so come in like manner."

Acts 1:11